What Is My Economy Like?

by Maureen Blaney Flietner

Editorial Offices: Glenview, Illinois • Parsippany, New Jersey • New York, New York

Sales Offices: Needham, Massachusetts • Duluth, Georgia • Glenview, Illinois
Coppell, Texas • Ontario, California • Mesa, Arizona

Working

Do you get an allowance from your parents? Do you get money as gifts or rewards?

If you work at a job, you earn money. The money you earn for working at a job is called income. You might provide services, jobs that one person does for another. You might provide goods, things that people grow or make and then sell.

It is important to learn about earning money. You will learn that most things are not free. You will learn to work for what you want and just how much you must work to pay for something.

If you learn how to be smart about your money, you can make your dreams come true.

What Do You Do With Your Money?

Many people love spending their money to buy things. There are many, many things to buy. Advertisements tell us so. Most children see more than twenty thousand advertisements on TV each year. Spending is only one thing you can do with your money.

Putting money into **savings** is also very important. When you save money, you keep it to use later. Saving money can be fun. Some children save their money in a piggybank, at a bank, or at a credit union. If you save your money you can see it add up!

For example, what would happen if you saved $2 each week? In 10 weeks, your savings would be $20. In a year, your savings would be $104. Money adds up! It is even more fun to save when you save for something special. What is something special you would like to save for?

People Have Basic Needs for Living

All of us have basic needs. A need is something you must have to live. The three basic needs that all people have are food, clothing, and shelter. Each of these costs money.

Many people do not have the money to pay for their needs. There are many reasons why they do not have enough money. Some people cannot find jobs. Some people are sick and cannot work. Some are old and some are children. Others help these people take care of their needs.

There Are Many Goods and Services Available

Businesses would like you to buy their goods and services. That is how they earn their money. They use advertisements to tell you about their goods and services. Advertisements are everywhere.

Are these goods and services something you need, or are these goods and services something you want? A want is something you would like to have but that you can live without. Sometimes it is hard to tell a need from a want. Even though fancy shoes or special jeans might seem like something you cannot live without, you can. They are wants, not needs.

Planning Ahead

Do you think about your next birthday? Do you think about fun things to do on your next summer vacation? Do you count the days until a favorite new book comes out?

When you think ahead, you are planning for the future. That is how you should think about your money.

When you think about the future and how you will use your money, you begin to plan. You think about what you would do with your money. Maybe your goal would be to buy something very special or to help someone in need. Maybe your goal would just be to save more money.

When you start to plan and have a goal, your money can add up fast.

Saving for a Bicycle	
Week 1	$10
Week 2	$10
Week 3	$10
Week 4	$10
Week 5	$10
Week 6	$10
Week 7	$10
Week 8	$10
Week 9	$10
Week 10	$10
Total	$100

Learn How to Use Your Money

When you plan how you would save and spend your income, you are making a **budget**. When you make a budget, you plan for your needs and your wants. You also plan for your future needs and future wants.

What if you wanted to make a budget to save for a bicycle that will cost $100? Let's suppose your allowance and job money add up to $10 a week.

If you saved all $10 of your money each week, it would take you 10 weeks to save enough to buy the bicycle. You would not be able to spend any of the money you earned. It might be hard at times, but you could do it.

What if you want to spend some money? If you save $5 each week and spend $5 each week, it would take you 20 weeks to save enough for the bicycle. When you change one part of the budget, such as savings, other parts of the budget also change.

In our sample budget, there is a choice: to spend or not to spend. Is what you want to buy important enough that you are willing to wait longer for the bicycle?

A Budget Can Work for Everyone

While a budget can help you spend and save your income, a budget can also help your family.

A family budget takes special planning. It must include food and clothes for all of the family members. It must include a home with heat, lights, and furniture. Maybe your family has plans for a car and gasoline and visits to the doctor or dentist. Can you think of other things that a family budget needs to include?

A family must use its income to pay for all of these needs and wants along with future needs and wants. Sometimes families need to find ways to save more or spend less.

Have Fun and Save Money Too!

Sometimes, when there is not enough income to pay for both wants and needs, you must look for ways to save money. You can save and have fun, too, by being a smart saver.

Instead of going to the movie theater, your family can rent a movie and make popcorn at home. Instead of going to the pizza restaurant, your family can save money by making a pizza at home. Your family can spend even less for food at the store by using coupons.

When you find ways to save, you often help people besides just you and your family. If you turn off the lights when you are not using them, you help save on the family electric bill and help the world in which you live. Much of the electricity for your lights comes from using **nonrenewable resources** such as coal and gas. Nonrenewable resources are often limited in their supply and cannot be made again. **Renewable resources** are the resources such as wind, water, and solar power that can be made available again. Save nonrenewable resources. Turn off the lights. Take a quick shower instead of a long one. Have a full load of clothes before you use a washer or dryer.

What Is an Economic Choice?

You make choices each day. Do you want to play outside or play inside? Which T-shirt do you want to wear? Do you want to have soup or a sandwich for lunch? There are other kinds of choices you make every day.

When you choose to buy one item instead of another, you are making an economic choice. When your family decides to buy a microwave oven instead of a TV, it is making an economic choice. When your community decides to build new roads instead of a new school, it is making an economic choice. There are many economic choices to be made.

Supply and Demand

Almost every year, there is one new item that everyone seems to talk about. There are stories about it on TV or in the newspapers. Everyone seems to want it, and you might see people waiting in long lines to buy one. Because there is such a **demand** for this item, the **supply** soon runs out.

Because you are smart about your money, you decide you really do not need or want this item. You think about the different things you have planned to do with your money. Spending your money on that particular item is not one of them. Let's suppose you decide to keep saving for that bicycle in our sample budget.

After a few months pass, you find that once again the popular item is in the stores. This time, there is no demand for it, and it is on sale. You decide that you might like to buy it now that it is on sale. You can still save some of your money and have the item too! By being smart with your money, you can spend and save.

Learn About Your Choices

Remember the budget that we planned for a bicycle? Let's suppose that you are still saving. While you save, you want to learn about bicycles and about your choices.

You can read books and magazine articles about bicycles. You can talk to classmates who have bicycles you like. You can visit stores to look at different bicycles and prices, and ask salespeople about the bicycles.

After you learn more, you decide to buy a bicycle from a company that makes the bicycles you like. The bicycle you choose is made by a company that has the capital resources, such as a building, tools, and machinery, to make bicycles. The company also has workers who know how to make these bicycles.

This company buys some parts it needs to make its bicycles from other countries. The bicycle company sells its bicycles to other countries. When businesses buy and sell with businesses in other countries, it is called international trade.

Money Moves Through Many Hands

In our sample bicycle budget, the big day finally arrives! The $100 has been saved and you are ready to buy your new bicycle. You learn that you have to pay a tax when you buy your bicycle, but your parents will pay that. The tax is money the government collects to pay for its services.

The bicycle company owner takes your money and pays the costs of making and selling that bicycle. The owner pays the people who sell bicycles for the company and the people who make the bicycles. The owner pays for the parts that were used to make the bicycle. The owner pays the tax to the government. The owner knows there will be a profit, or extra money left over. The owner keeps the profit. That is how the bicycle company earns money.

As you learned, money is earned, money is spent, and money is saved. You earn money by working. You save some of it, and you spend some of it. Other people also earn money. They save money to buy things they will want and need, both now and in the future.

We all depend on each other for many things. You depend on your family for your food, shelter, and clothing. You depend on teachers to help you learn. All people depend on other people. When we depend, or rely, on each other, it is called interdependence.

Making Wise Choices

You saved enough money to buy a bicycle in our sample budget. You can save and buy things you want with a real budget. All you have to do is make a budget, earn income, and plan how you want to save and spend.

Some people are not educated savers and may not know how to make a budget. They may spend everything they earn. Money will not be there when they need it.

You know how to make a budget. You are starting to learn how to be smart with your money. If you are careful with your money, you will have enough money for your needs and your wants. You will reach your goals.

Glossary

budget a plan for your income, savings, and spending

demand the number of goods or services that people want and will buy at a given price

nonrenewable resources supplies that cannot be made again

renewable resources supplies that can be created naturally

savings money you have kept for future use

supply the number of goods or services that producers are willing to make at a given price